TO

FROM

LITTLE DREAMS

♡ OF ♡

HAPPINESS

Illustrations by Julia Glynn Smith

**Andrews McMeel
Publishing**

Kansas City

CONFETTI MOMENTS

S P R I N G

H A P P I N E S S

So many daffodils

And no basket

Large enough for April

The iridescent butterfly

That settles for an instant

And then moves on

CONFETTI MOMENT

★ I ★

The first spring visitor

Thousands of scarlet ruffles
Each catching the light
Thousands of dancing poppies
Each catching the wind

Enough wind to lift a kite...

Spring cleaning

That finishing touch...

C O N F E T T I   M O M E N T

★ 2 ★

Finally
The first
"no coat day"

So much cherry blossom

The sky is overwhelmed

By pink

SUMMER

HAPPINESS

When my bicycle

Takes me along

The sunflower-lined road

Home-grown vegetables

CONFETTI MOMENT

★ 3 ★

Away on a day trip...

All that sun in the fig
At the first bite
The whole summer
Bursts in your mouth

Curling your toes in the warm sand

All the way to the cool water

CONFETTI MOMENT

★ 4 ★

Dark summer fruits

In a still-

steaming pie

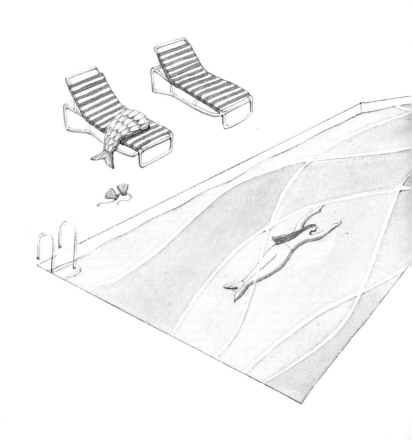

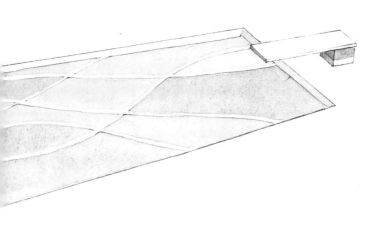

A skinny-dip

Sharing a shooting star

With a friend

AUTUMN

HAPPINESS

An infinity of apples

An autumn full of pies

CONFETTI MOMENT

★ 5 ★

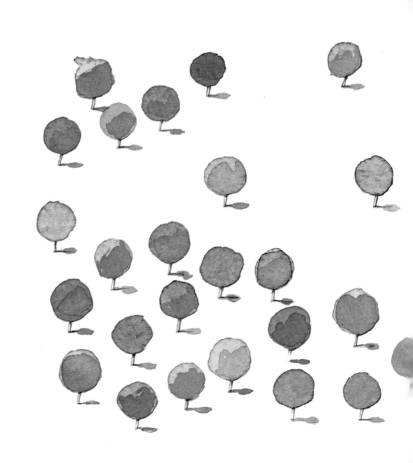

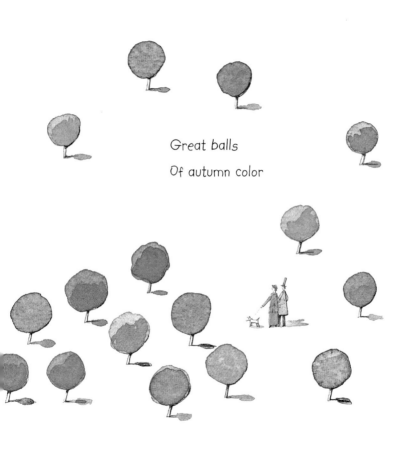

Great balls
Of autumn color

Home-baked anything!

Harvest moon...

So fat

So round

Summer's last

Beachball

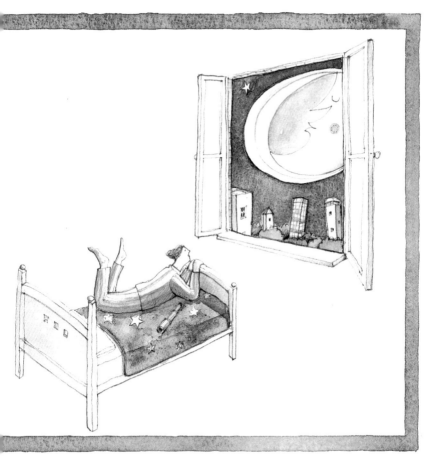

C O N F E T T I   M O M E N T

★ 6 ★

Caught-up
In a confetti
Of October leaves

Pumpkin faces

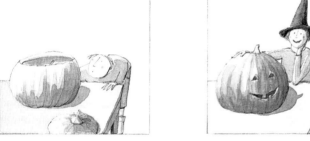

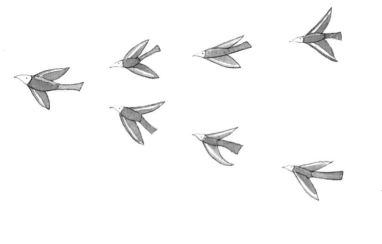

So many V's in the sky

All in the same direction

All going somewhere

WINTER

HAPPINESS

Fireside...

Friends...

And a long evening ahead

The quiet white of winter's

first snowfall...

A smooth glide
On clear ice

The perfect moment

The perfect decoration

Palm trees at Christmas

C O N F E T T I   M O M E N T

★ 8 ★

A bath by candlelight

Valentine surprises

ANYTIME

HAPPINESS

After a long day
That special welcome home

The new sheets are
Clean and white...
A bed of fresh snow

CONFETTI MOMENT

★ 9 ★

Stepping out

In new shoes

No one
In the kitchen
And the rich chocolate
Icing is left in the bowl

Fresh-faced sun

A cascade of golden notes

And breakfast in bed

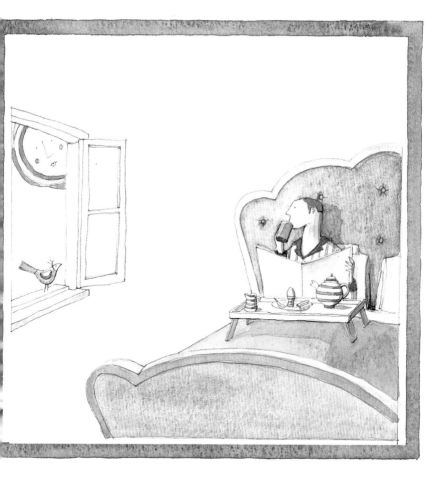

CONFETTI MOMENT

★ 10 ★

That silken purr

Curving round and round

Your ankles

Getting an "A"

Julia Glynn Smith worked as an architect and designer before illustrating her first book. She lives in Islington, London, but is never happier than when stepping out with a new map in hand and new places to discover.

First published by MQ Publications Limited
254–258 Goswell Road, London EC1V 7RL

Copyright © MQ Publications Limited 2000
Illustrations © Julia Glynn Smith 2000
Text © Lulu Colebrooke and Zoe Westgate 2000

ISBN: 0-7407-0549-0

Library of Congress Catalog Card Number: 99-67991

1 3 5 7 9 0 8 6 4 2

Printed and bound in China